ENHANCE YOUR EFFICIENCY TO ACHIEVE YOUR GOALS

Ram Asare Shukla

Some sample scenarios in this book are fictitious. Any similarity to actual persons, living or dead, is coincidental.

Introduction

This book is for anyone willing and craving to achieve more in lesser time, with lesser resources and yet not compromising on quality. This book will help you with tips and tricks to enhance your efficiency.

Contents

INTRODUCTION

TO

EFFICIENCY

Efficiency

Asha was late to work when she noticed that about 15 of her colleagues, who all resided in the same locality came to office late that day. She knew it was due to the poor public transport connectivity, which gets even worse during rainy season. During the lunch break she happened to speak with few of them and decided to take this issue with the company's Transit Team. Understanding the employees plight Transit Manager agreed to provide a Minibus to accommodate all 15 employees from that locality. Asha's efforts resulted in lesser transit time and trouble for her colleagues. They were all able to come to office on time and leave on time as well. Less exhaustion and happiness lead to increased focus on work. Their performance matrix numbers showed increased productivity at work.

Taking Asha's example one might wonder- are there other ways as well to increase the performance of an individual at workplace or at home? Are there ways to shorten the effort? Or time taken? If the answer is YES, you are on the right track of enhancing your efficiency.

The term "Efficiency" has been excessively used in offices nowadays. This term might sound difficult to understand at first. However, the concept of how it works is known to mankind since time immemorial. We have- on numerous occasions tried to shorten the time taken to do a job or allocated people to do work based on their area of expertise. All these ways are nothing but ways to increase efficiency.

Now, in today's fast-growing world we need to optimize our efforts and resources to achieve the results faster without compromising on quality. Therefore, the emphasis of enhancing efficiency comes into picture.

It involves adopting strategies and practices that help you and your team accomplish more in less time.

It is a measure of how well a system, process, or individual performs in terms of producing the desired results while minimizing inefficiencies, unnecessary steps, or resource usage. Efficiency is a key concept in various domains, including business, manufacturing, technology, and personal productivity.

Some of the important aspects of efficiency are:

Optimization of Resources: Efficient systems or processes aim to make the best use of available resources, such as time, money, energy, and materials. This involves minimizing waste and ensuring that resources are utilized effectively.

Streamlined Processes: Efficiency often involves streamlining processes by eliminating unnecessary steps or bottlenecks. This helps create a more straightforward and effective workflow.

Time Management: Time efficiency is a crucial component. Efficient individuals or organizations manage their time effectively, prioritize tasks, and avoid unnecessary delays to achieve their goals.

Cost Reduction: Efficient operations can lead to cost savings. By identifying and eliminating inefficiencies, organizations can reduce expenses and improve their overall financial performance.

Productivity Improvement: An efficient system is associated with higher productivity, meaning it can achieve more output with the same input or achieve the same output with fewer resources.

Quality Maintenance: True efficiency doesn't compromise quality. Efficient processes should maintain or enhance the quality of the final product or service.

Continuous Improvement: Efficiency is an ongoing process. Successful organizations and individuals continuously seek ways to improve their processes, adapt to changing circumstances, and stay ahead in their respective fields.

Balancing Efficiency and Effectiveness: While efficiency focuses on doing things right, effectiveness considers whether the right things are being done. Striking a balance between efficiency and effectiveness is crucial for sustainable success.

Efficiency is a critical factor in achieving organizational goals, meeting customer expectations, and maintaining competitiveness. Striving for efficiency involves a constant commitment to improvement, adaptability, and a keen understanding of how resources can be optimized to achieve the best possible outcomes.

GOALS

AND

IMPORTANT

TASKS

Goals and Important Tasks

Narayan, always aimed to become an Officer in Civil Services. His goal was clear. He wanted to make sure that he becomes an officer before the age of 25. He graduated in Bachelor of Arts with majors in History. He wanted to appear for the Civil Services exam with History as his subject. He always excelled in all his exam. He also made sure to maintain a proper diet and a healthy lifestyle. He always dressed smartly. Every minute of his schedule was properly planned and executed wonderfully. All this helped him in clearing PRELIMS and MAINS Exam along with the Interview with flying colours.

He was able to become an IAS Office because his Goal was clear. He prioritized his studies and prepared well for the role. He had also kept a time restriction. In short, his Goal was SMART. Now, you might wonder what does that stand for?

Setting clear goals is a crucial step in achieving efficiency, whether in personal or professional endeavours. Clear goals provide direction, motivation, and a framework for measuring progress.

Here are some key steps to set clear goals for achieving efficiency:

Define Your Objectives: Clearly articulate what you want to achieve. Be specific and avoid vague statements. For example, instead of saying, "Increase sales," specify, "Increase monthly sales by 20% within the next quarter."

Make Them SMART:

Use the SMART criteria for goal setting:

Specific: Clearly define the goal.

Measurable: Establish measurable criteria to track progress.

Achievable: Ensure the goal is realistic and attainable.

Relevant: Align the goal with broader objectives.

Time-bound: Set a deadline for achieving the goal.

Break Down Larger Goals: If you have a big goal, break it down into smaller, more manageable tasks. This makes it easier to track progress and prevents feeling overwhelmed.

 Prioritize: Identify the most critical goals and prioritize them based on their impact. This helps you focus on what matters most and allocate resources efficiently.

Create Action Plans: Develop detailed action plans outlining the steps you need to take to achieve each goal. Break down tasks into actionable items with deadlines.

Allocate Resources: Determine the resources required to achieve your goals, such as time, money, and personnel. Ensure that these resources are available and allocated appropriately.

Monitor and Evaluate: Regularly monitor your progress and evaluate whether you are on track to meet your goals. If needed, adjust your strategies or action plans.

Communicate Goals: Share your goals with relevant stakeholders, whether they are team members, colleagues, or family. Clear communication ensures everyone is on the same page and can contribute to the overall efficiency.

Celebrate Milestones: Acknowledge and celebrate achievements along the way. This boosts morale and motivation, making it easier to stay focused on the larger objectives.

Review and Revise: Regularly review your goals, assess your progress, and be willing to revise them if necessary. Circumstances and priorities may change, requiring adjustments to your goals.

Learn from Feedback: Seek feedback from yourself and others involved in the goal-setting process. Use this feedback to learn and improve your goal setting and efficiency strategies.

By setting clear goals following these principles, you create a roadmap for success and enhance your ability to achieve efficiency in various aspects of your life or work.

TIME

MANAGEMENT

Time Management

Shruti works as a Personal Assistant in CEO Office of an MNC. Her work resolves around managing CEO's calendar, meetings, notes, reviewing speeches, writing emails etc. In short, it's not limited to one set of tasks. Also, each of her tasks requires her to be absolutely on time. A delay in schedule or work can impact the CEO's reputation along with the troubles in the company. She does her job dedicatedly without missing on any Tasks or deadline.

To achieve the best of her ability to do the job, she uses a lot of Time Management tools like calendars, planners, or productivity apps to schedule and track her work. She breaks down larger tasks into smaller, more manageable chunks to keep a track of time and effort spent on them. Remember that effective time management is a skill that develops over time. Experiment with different techniques to find what works best for you and be willing to adapt your approach as needed. Consistency and self-awareness are key components of successful time management.

Set Clear Goals: Clearly define your short-term and long-term goals. Knowing what you want to achieve helps prioritize tasks and focus your efforts.

Prioritize Tasks: Identify tasks based on their urgency and importance. Use methods like the Eisenhower Matrix, categorizing tasks as urgent-important, important-not urgent, urgent-not important, and neither urgent nor important.

Create a To-Do List: Make a daily or weekly to-do list. Break down larger tasks into smaller, manageable steps. Update the list regularly and cross off completed tasks.

Use Time Blocks: Allocate specific time blocks for different types of activities. This helps prevent multitasking and allows you to concentrate on one task at a time.

Set Time Limits: Assign a specific time limit to each task. This creates a sense of urgency and helps prevent tasks from expanding to fill available time.

Eliminate Time Wasters: Identify and minimize activities that waste your time, such as excessive social media use, unnecessary meetings, or procrastination. Be mindful of distractions and find ways to mitigate them.

Batch Similar Tasks: Group similar tasks together and tackle them during designated time blocks. This minimizes context switching and improves overall efficiency.

Learn to Say "No": Recognize your limits and be selective about taking on additional responsibilities. Saying no, when necessary, helps you maintain focus on your priorities.

Use Technology Wisely: Leverage productivity tools and apps to streamline tasks and manage your schedule. Calendar apps, task management tools, and reminders can be valuable assets.

Take Breaks: Regular breaks can help maintain focus and prevent burnout. Use techniques like the Pomodoro Technique, where you work for a focused 25-minute period and then take a 5-minute break.

Delegate Tasks: Delegate tasks that can be handled by others. This allows you to concentrate on tasks that require your specific skills and expertise.

Learn to Delegate: If you are working in a team, delegate tasks based on team members' strengths. Trust your team to handle responsibilities, and focus on your areas of expertise.

Review and Reflect: Regularly assess how you are spending your time. Identify patterns and adjust your time management strategies based on what works best for you.

Continuous Improvement: Embrace a mindset of continuous improvement. Regularly assess and refine your time management techniques to adapt to changing circumstances and priorities.

DISTRACTIONS

Eliminating distractions

Rohan, an investment banker, always aimed to be the best at his trade. He was well educated and had a fantastic network. He was Smart, Intelligent, and Impressionable young man. He wanted to do better than his childhood friends or colleagues. Even though he had a lot of good qualities, he was still not considered a reliable Investment Banker. He focused on building network but didn't focus on giving the returns his clients were looking for. He attended a lot of parties, events, games etc. After coming home, he opens social media sites and goes through his friends and colleagues profiles to compare his lifestyle with theirs, in terms of vacations, clothes, luxury brands etc.

Now you might wonder what Rohan must change in his life to become more efficient with his work and become a successful Investment Banker. Most of you might have already guessed it.

Eliminating distractions is a key strategy for increasing productivity. Identify and minimize distractions such as unnecessary meetings, notifications, or social media. Also, consider implementing focused work periods without interruptions.

Here are specific actions you can take to minimize distractions and create a more focused work environment:

Designate a Dedicated Workspace: Create a specific area for work that is free from distractions. Ideally, this space should be separate from areas associated with leisure or other non-work activities.

Turn Off Notifications: Disable non-essential notifications on your devices, including your phone, computer, and smartwatch. This prevents constant interruptions from emails, messages, and social media.

Establish a Schedule: Set specific work hours and stick to a consistent schedule. This routine helps train your mind to focus during dedicated work periods and can reduce the likelihood of distractions.

Use "Do Not Disturb" Mode: Activate the "Do Not Disturb" mode on your devices during focused work sessions. This silences incoming calls, messages, and notifications, allowing you to concentrate without interruption.

Prioritize Tasks: Identify and prioritize your most important tasks. By focusing on high-priority items first, you can reduce the impact of distractions on critical work.

Batch Similar Tasks: Group similar tasks together and tackle them during specific time blocks. This minimizes the need for constant context switching, which can be distracting.

Communicate Boundaries: Clearly communicate your work hours and boundaries to family members, roommates, or colleagues. Let them know when you need uninterrupted time to focus on work.

Use Headphones or White Noise: Headphones can help block out ambient noise, and playing soothing background music or white noise can create a focused environment.

Limit Access to Social Media: Set specific times for checking and responding to social media. Consider using website blockers or apps that limit your access to these platforms during work hours.

Create a To-Do List: Develop a daily or weekly to-do list that outlines your tasks. This provides a roadmap for your day and helps you stay on track.

Minimize Multitasking: Focus on one task at a time rather than trying to juggle multiple activities simultaneously. Multitasking can decrease overall efficiency and increase the likelihood of distractions.

Delegate and Outsource: Delegate tasks that can be handled by others. This allows you to concentrate on tasks that require your specific skills and expertise.

Use Tools for Focus: Explore productivity tools and apps designed to help you stay focused. Some tools provide features like website blockers, time tracking, and focus timers.

Establish Clear Communication Channels: Clearly define communication channels for urgent matters. This can reduce the frequency of interruptions while still allowing for important messages to reach you.

Practice Mindfulness Techniques: Incorporate mindfulness practices such as meditation or deep breathing exercises into your routine. These techniques can help you stay present and focused.

Consistency is key when implementing these strategies. Experiment with different approaches to find what works best for you and adjust as needed. Creating a distraction-free environment contributes significantly to increased productivity and overall work satisfaction.

RESPONSIBILITY

Delegating Responsibility

Arun recently got a promotion in his job. He became a Supervisory Expert on the Healthcare Domain. He was thrilled. His manager started asking him for various reports. He was asked to join multiple meetings and events. Due to all this sometimes he was not able to provide guidance to his team or supervise their work on the domain. He was upset that he was not able to give time to his team.

To fulfil the gap, he thought of asking one of his team members to take care of the team in his absence. He felt a senior team member with years of experience would be able to take responsibility. So, then he asked Kavita to take up this responsibility. Now, Arun can focus on his team as well as managerial events. Kavita on the other hand feels empowered and recognized for the years of service she has delivered.

Delegating responsibility is a powerful strategy for achieving efficiency in both personal and professional settings. By distributing tasks to others, you can leverage the strengths and expertise of your team, enhance productivity, and focus on high-priority activities.

Here are some tips for effective delegation:

Understand Your Team's Strengths: Assess the skills and strengths of your team members. Understanding their capabilities helps you assign tasks that align with their expertise.

Clearly Define Tasks and Objectives: Clearly articulate the tasks you want to delegate and the desired outcomes. Provide clear instructions, expectations, and any necessary resources.

Choose the Right Person for the Task: Match tasks with the skills and interests of your team members. Consider their expertise, experience, and workload when delegating responsibilities.

Communicate Clearly: Ensure that your communication is clear and concise. Clearly explain the purpose, importance, and expectations associated with the delegated task.

Establish Trust: Trust is crucial for effective delegation. Trust your team members to handle the assigned responsibilities and be available for guidance and support as needed.

Set Realistic Deadlines: Establish realistic deadlines for delegated tasks. Consider the complexity of the task and the workload of the team member to whom it is assigned.

Encourage Questions and Feedback: Create an open line of communication for questions and feedback. Encourage team members to seek clarification or provide input to ensure a smooth delegation process.

Provide Resources and Support: Ensure that your team has the necessary resources and support to complete delegated tasks successfully. This may include access to information, tools, or training.

Monitor Progress: Regularly check in on the progress of delegated tasks. This allows you to provide guidance, address any issues that may arise, and ensure that the work aligns with expectations.

Acknowledge Achievements: Recognize and appreciate the efforts and achievements of team members who successfully complete delegated tasks. Positive feedback reinforces a sense of accomplishment and motivation.

Be Open to Delegating Authority: Delegating responsibility may also involve delegating decision-making authority. Trust your team to make decisions within their areas of expertise, empowering them to take ownership.

Learn from Delegation Experiences: Reflect on your delegation experiences. Identify what worked well and areas for improvement. Use this feedback to enhance your future delegation strategies.

Encourage Collaboration: Foster a collaborative environment where team members can support each other. Delegating tasks can promote teamwork and strengthen the overall capabilities of the group.

Delegate Strategically: Consider the long-term development of your team when delegating tasks. Use delegation as a tool for skill development and succession planning.

Be Flexible: Be open to adjusting your delegation approach based on the evolving needs of the team and the organization. Flexibility is key to successful delegation.

Efficient delegation requires a balance between trust, clear communication, and ongoing support. By mastering the art of delegation, you can optimize your team's performance and contribute to overall organizational efficiency.

COMMUNICATION

Improve Communication

Ujwal is an excellent coder at a Start-up firm. His codes are like magic. He is proficient at his job. He is a team player and is admired by his team. One day Sushil, his manager, asked him to send out an email with the details of the upcoming Techathon. He sends out the details and everybody with coding background applied.

On the day of the event, most people didn't turn up in the auditorium for the Techathon. Sushil got furious and looked at Ujwal. Ujwal was also confused. Then he looked at the email again and realised that time of event was wrongly mentioned. Instead of 8 AM, the email had it 8 PM. Such small detail, if overlooked can cause issues. Do not assume that people will understand. Pay attention and make it correct in the beginning itself.

Improving communication is essential for enhancing efficiency in various aspects of life, whether it's in the workplace, personal relationships, or within a team. Use clear and concise communication methods. Utilize project management tools and collaboration platforms to streamline communication.

Here are some strategies to improve communication and increase overall efficiency:

Establish Clear Objectives: Clearly define the goals and objectives of a project or task. When everyone understands the purpose and desired outcomes, communication becomes more focused and effective.

Use Clear and Concise Language: Avoid ambiguity and use straightforward language. Clearly articulate your ideas, instructions, and expectations to minimize misunderstandings.

Active Listening: Practice active listening by fully engaging with what others are saying. Avoid interrupting and ask clarifying questions to ensure a complete understanding.

Choose the Right Communication Channels: Select the most appropriate communication channel for a given message. Some information is better conveyed through face-to-face meetings, while others may be suitable for email or instant messaging.

Provide Regular Updates: Keep team members informed about progress, changes, or updates. Regular communication ensures that everyone is on the same page and reduces the risk of misunderstandings.

Encourage Open Communication: Create an environment that encourages open and honest communication. Team members should feel comfortable sharing their thoughts, ideas, and concerns without fear of reprisal.

Use Visual Aids: Supplement verbal communication with visual aids such as charts, graphs, or diagrams. Visuals can enhance understanding and make complex information more accessible.

Set Clear Expectations: Clearly communicate expectations regarding roles, responsibilities, and deadlines. When everyone is on the same page, tasks are more likely to be completed efficiently.

Provide Constructive Feedback: Offer feedback that is specific, constructive, and focused on improvement. This helps individuals understand their strengths and areas for development.

Use Technology Wisely: Leverage communication tools and technology to facilitate collaboration. This includes project management software, messaging apps, video conferencing, and collaborative platforms.

Clarify Assumptions: Address assumptions and potential misunderstandings early on. Encourage team members to seek clarification if they are unsure about any aspect of a project or task.

Establish Regular Meetings: Hold regular team meetings to discuss progress, challenges, and upcoming tasks. Meetings provide an opportunity for open communication and collaboration.

Be Mindful of Non-Verbal Communication: Pay attention to non-verbal cues such as body language and facial expressions. These can convey important information and emotions that may not be expressed verbally.

Cultivate a Positive Tone: Maintain a positive and respectful tone in written and verbal communication. A positive tone fosters a collaborative and supportive environment.

Continuous Improvement: Regularly assess the effectiveness of communication within the team or organization. Seek feedback, identify areas for improvement, and adjust your communication strategies accordingly.

By focusing on clear, open, and effective communication, you can significantly enhance efficiency and collaboration within any group or organization. Continuous improvement and adaptability to different communication needs are key to long-term success.

REPETITIVE

TASKS

Automating Repetitive Tasks

Arundhatti works as a Customer Service Executive in an MNC. One of the tasks she does, is to reset the password of her clients access to their website. But every time she does a reset of Password, she must send out an email to the customer with Username and Password, along with some company defined statements. So, to optimize her time, she prepared a template, which can used in all her emails. She even shared this template with all her teammates making their work easier. During one of the meetings, she suggested management to build an integration to send out Automatic Emails every time they reset the password for clients.

Arundhatti was appreciated for giving a wonderful solution. Soon, the idea was implemented. She was able to automate a repetitive task and focus on other tasks better.

Automating repetitive tasks is a powerful strategy for increasing efficiency, saving time, and reducing errors. Identify repetitive and time-consuming tasks that can be automated. Explore tools and software that can help automate routine processes.

Here are steps and approaches you can take to automate tasks effectively:

Identify Repetitive Tasks: List tasks that are repetitive and time-consuming. These could include data entry, file organization, email responses, or any other routine activities that don't require complex decision-making.

Prioritize Tasks for Automation: Assess which repetitive tasks have the most significant impact on your productivity when automated. Prioritize those that are resource-intensive and occur frequently.

Research Automation Tools: Explore tools and software that can help automate specific tasks. There are various automation platforms, such as Zapier, IFTTT, or Microsoft Power Automate, that can streamline workflows and integrate different applications.

Leverage Built-in Features: Many software applications come with built-in features for automation. Explore the functionalities of the tools you already use to see if they offer automation capabilities.

Start Small: Begin by automating smaller, less complex tasks. This allows you to familiarize yourself with automation tools and gain confidence before tackling more intricate processes.

Create Workflows: Design workflows that outline the steps of a task from start to finish. This helps you understand the process and identify where automation can be applied.

Use Scripting and Macros: For tasks that require a series of repetitive actions, consider using scripting or macros. This is especially useful in applications like Microsoft Excel or Google Sheets.

Integrate Applications: Automate the transfer of data between different applications by integrating them. For example, you can connect your email marketing platform with your CRM system to automatically update customer records.

Set Triggers: Automation tools often use triggers to initiate actions. Set up triggers based on specific conditions, such as time, data changes, or user inputs, to start automated processes.

Test and Iterate: Before fully implementing automation, test your workflows to ensure they function as intended. Iterate and make adjustments based on the results of your testing.

Implement Artificial Intelligence (AI): Explore AI-powered solutions for more complex tasks. Machine learning algorithms can be trained to perform tasks that require decision-making based on patterns and data analysis.

Secure Data and Processes: Ensure that the automation processes you implement are secure. Protect sensitive data and regularly update security measures to prevent vulnerabilities.

Train Teams: If automation is implemented in a team setting, provide training to team members on how to use and interact with automated processes. This ensures a smooth transition and maximizes the benefits of automation.

Monitor and Optimize: Regularly monitor automated processes to identify any issues or areas for improvement. Optimize workflows based on feedback and changes in business requirements.

Scale Gradually: As you gain confidence and experience with automation, gradually scale its implementation across more tasks and processes. This can lead to significant time savings and efficiency gains over time.

Automating repetitive tasks not only increases efficiency but also allows individuals and teams to focus on more valuable and strategic activities. Regularly reassess your processes to identify new opportunities for automation as technology evolves and business needs change.

LEARNING

Continuous Learning

Mohan, a Research Engineer in R&D Department of an MNC, has got promoted recently and has been assigned on to a Machine Learning Project. His colleagues wondered as to when did Mohan get time to learn about ML. He had earlier worked on Propulsion related Projects.

Looks like he use to attend additional courses on Machine Learning from past one year. He is an enthusiast who likes to learn about latest technologies to keep himself informed and to excel on the projects he takes. Everyone on his team agreed that its continuous learning which helps one to be efficient.

Continuous learning is a powerful strategy to enhance work efficiency, keeping your skills and knowledge up-to-date and relevant in a rapidly changing work environment. It is important to stay updated on the latest tools and techniques in your field. Always encourage a culture of continuous learning within your team.

Here are specific ways continuous learning can contribute to increased efficiency at work:

Adaptation to Change: Continuous learning helps you stay abreast of industry trends, technological advancements, and changes in your field. This adaptability ensures that you can navigate transitions and embrace new tools and methodologies efficiently.

Skill Development: Learning new skills or refining existing ones makes you more proficient in your role. This increased competence leads to quicker and more effective task execution.

Problem-Solving Abilities: Acquiring a diverse range of knowledge and skills enhances your problem-solving abilities. You can approach challenges with a broader perspective and identify innovative solutions more efficiently.

Time Management: Learning how to manage your time effectively is a skill that contributes directly to work efficiency. Time management courses and strategies can help you prioritize tasks and accomplish more in less time.

Enhanced Productivity Tools: Continuous learning allows you to discover and master new productivity tools and software that can streamline your workflow. This can result in time savings and increased efficiency in your daily tasks.

Project Management Skills: Developing project management skills through continuous learning helps you plan, execute, and complete projects more efficiently. This includes skills in task delegation, resource allocation, and meeting deadlines.

Communication Skills: Improving your communication skills can lead to more effective collaboration, reducing misunderstandings and streamlining the exchange of information in the workplace.

Leadership Development: Continuous learning in leadership and management practices can enhance your ability to lead teams and projects efficiently. Strong leadership contributes to a more organized and motivated work environment.

Embracing New Technologies: In many industries, technology evolves rapidly. Continuous learning allows you to adapt to and leverage new technologies, increasing your efficiency in using the latest tools and systems.

Networking Opportunities: Engaging in continuous learning often involves attending workshops, conferences, or online forums. Networking with professionals in your field can open opportunities for collaboration and shared insights, enhancing your overall efficiency.

Professional Development: Ongoing professional development ensures that you are equipped with the latest knowledge and best practices. This helps you perform your tasks with greater proficiency and a deeper understanding of your industry.

Job Satisfaction and Motivation: Continuous learning can contribute to job satisfaction by providing a sense of growth and accomplishment. Motivated and satisfied employees are often more productive and efficient in their roles.

Risk Mitigation: Staying informed about industry regulations, compliance requirements, and ethical standards through continuous learning helps mitigate the risk of errors or non-compliance, promoting a smoother workflow.

Efficient Decision-Making: Learning about decision-making frameworks and strategies can enhance your ability to make well-informed decisions more efficiently, avoiding delays and improving overall workflow.

Focus on Lifelong Learning: Adopting a mindset of lifelong learning ensures that you are continually seeking new knowledge and skills, making you more adaptable, resilient, and efficient in the face of changing work environments.

Embracing continuous learning is an investment in your personal and professional growth, contributing to increased efficiency, effectiveness, and overall success in your work.

MEETINGS

Streamline Meetings

Rana works as a Technology Lead in Software Development team of an MNC. He handles a team of about ten people. He is considered smart, professional and an excellent lead by his team members. He is often noted for being precise and practical in his approach towards to any problem. Even his meetings are very precise.

His colleagues or other Tech Leads wonder how his virtual meetings are so short. How does he make sure all the points are covered and if the team has understood the assignment. So on and so forth were their questions.

Rana always made sure the objective and agenda of the meeting was informed well in advance. He kept his meetings short, to discuss only the important points. He also created a healthy environment where all his teammates felt comfortable asking questions. These are some of the points Rana kept in mind to make sure his meetings were as effective as possible.

Streamlining meetings is crucial for maximizing efficiency, ensuring that time is used productively, and preventing unnecessary delays.

Here are strategies to streamline meetings and increase overall efficiency:

Set Clear Objectives: Clearly define the purpose and objectives of the meeting. Ensure that everyone understands what needs to be achieved and focus only on essential topics.

Create an Agenda: Develop a detailed agenda outlining the topics to be discussed and the time allocated to each. Share the agenda in advance to allow participants to prepare.

Invite Only Essential Participants: Include only those individuals whose presence is necessary for the meeting. This minimizes interruptions and ensures that discussions remain focused.

Set a Time Limit: Establish a specific time limit for the meeting and adhere to it strictly. This encourages participants to stay focused and ensures that the meeting does not extend beyond what is necessary.

Start and End on Time: Begin the meeting punctually and end it on time. This shows respect for participants' schedules and reinforces the importance of staying on track.

Utilize Technology Wisely: Leverage technology to facilitate efficient communication. Use video conferencing, collaboration tools, and shared documents to streamline discussions and decision-making.

Pre-Circulate Materials: Share relevant documents, reports, or materials in advance. This allows participants to review information before the meeting, reducing the need for lengthy explanations during the session.

Encourage Participation: Create an environment where all participants feel comfortable sharing their input. Encourage active participation and contributions from everyone to avoid unnecessary follow-up discussions.

Limit Agenda Items: Keep the agenda focused on a limited number of high-priority items. This prevents meetings from becoming overly long and ensures that each topic receives adequate attention.

Assign Responsibilities: Clearly assign responsibilities for action items or tasks that arise during the meeting. This helps prevent misunderstandings and ensures accountability.

Follow Up Promptly: Send out meeting minutes and follow-up actions promptly after the meeting. This reinforces accountability and keeps participants informed about decisions and next steps.

Stand-Up Meetings: For brief updates or quick check-ins, consider using stand-up meetings. The physical discomfort of standing encourages brevity and helps keep the meeting focused.

Use a Parking Lot: If tangential topics arise during the meeting, note them in a "parking lot" for discussion at a later time. This prevents derailing the current agenda.

Evaluate the Necessity of the Meeting: Before scheduling a meeting, assess whether it's truly necessary. If the same objectives can be achieved through alternative means, such as email updates or collaboration tools, consider skipping the meeting.

Seek Feedback: Regularly gather feedback from participants about the efficiency of meetings. Use this input to identify areas for improvement and refine your meeting processes.

By implementing these strategies, you can streamline meetings, make them more efficient, and ensure that participants' time is used productively. This not only enhances overall workplace efficiency but also contributes to a positive and respectful organizational culture.

BREAKS AND REST

Encourage Breaks and Rest:

Rohit once joined a software development firm as an Executive. He was new to the corporate world. He was enthusiastic and loved his job. He would also take up a lot of project and non-project activities. His love for his job became so much so that he started coming to office even over the weekend to do either some courses or work on any code. Working on weekends was not common in his team as they were still executives.

His manager, Suresh, happened to visit office on one of the weekends and noticed Rohit working on a code. He was initially impressed but when Rohit informed that he had been coming to office every weekend, Suresh was not happy. Suresh asked Rohit to slow down and take rest to not have burnout early in his career. He asked Rohit to do either Laundry, play games, meet up friends or take time to relax. He told Rohit the importance of Work- Life Balance. Rohit listened to his manager and followed his advice. It has been 15 years that he has been working with the organization and still loves his job.

Absolutely, breaks and rest play a crucial role in maintaining and increasing efficiency. Short breaks can help refresh the mind and increase overall productivity. Make sure to encourage a healthy work-life balance to prevent burnout.

Here are several reasons why incorporating breaks and rest into your routine is essential for overall well-being and productivity:

Physical and Mental Refreshment: Taking breaks allows your body and mind to recharge.

Stepping away from work for a short period helps prevent fatigue and maintains optimal cognitive function.

Improved Focus and Concentration: Continuous work without breaks can lead to diminishing returns in terms of focus and concentration. Short breaks provide an opportunity to reset and return to tasks with renewed attention.

Enhanced Creativity and Problem-Solving: Breaks stimulate creativity and can lead to new perspectives on problems. Stepping away from a challenging task allows your brain to process information in the background, often resulting in innovative solutions.

Reduced Stress Levels: Breaks help manage stress levels by providing moments of relaxation. Persistent stress can negatively impact efficiency, and regular breaks act as a buffer against burnout.

Prevention of Burnout: Taking regular breaks helps prevent burnout, a state of emotional, physical, and mental exhaustion caused by prolonged stress. Burnout can significantly hinder efficiency and overall job performance.

Improved Health and Well-being: Breaks contribute to overall health and well-being. Physical activities during breaks, such as stretching or walking, can improve circulation, reduce muscle tension, and promote a healthier lifestyle.

Maintained Energy Levels: Breaks help regulate energy levels throughout the day. Short breaks can prevent the slump in energy that often occurs during long stretches of continuous work.

Enhanced Learning and Memory: Rest periods are essential for effective learning and memory consolidation. They allow the brain to process and store information gained during work periods.

Positive Impact on Mood: Taking breaks can have a positive impact on your mood. Engaging in activities you enjoy during breaks can boost morale, contributing to a more positive and productive work environment.

Encourages Social Interaction: Breaks provide opportunities for social interaction with colleagues. Socializing can foster a sense of community and teamwork, positively influencing the overall work atmosphere.

Promotes Healthy Habits: Regular breaks create a structured rhythm to your day, encouraging healthy habits such as hydration, healthy snacking, and proper meals, which contribute to sustained energy levels.

Enhances Time Management: Taking breaks helps improve time management by allowing you to assess progress and reassess priorities. It can prevent wasted time on unproductive tasks by providing moments of reflection.

Optimizes Cognitive Function: Continuous work can lead to cognitive fatigue. Breaks optimize cognitive function by preventing mental exhaustion and maintaining the brain's ability to process information effectively.

Supports Work-Life Balance: Integrating breaks into your workday contributes to a healthier work-life balance. Recognizing the importance of both work and personal time fosters a more sustainable and fulfilling lifestyle.

Increased Job Satisfaction: Employees who have the flexibility to take breaks often experience increased job satisfaction. This positive sentiment can lead to higher levels of engagement and commitment to their work.

Remember that the optimal structure and duration of breaks may vary from person to person. It's important to experiment and find a routine that suits your individual needs and preferences while aligning with the demands of your work.

FEEDBACK

Regular Feedback

Usha, works as a Fashion Designer with a major Fashion Brand. She has keen interest in making sure her customers love her dresses. Her idea of fashion is Comfort with Elegance. She had made a name for herself in the market as someone who makes comfortable stylish dresses, not necessary a trendy dress.

One afternoon, she thought to herself, what if she makes trendy, stylish and yet comfortable dresses. The idea in her mind was to become a trend setter. Her Brand Manager, Kunal, asked her to continue with her area of expertise, but she argued. Kunal finally agreed and let her experiment. She made many dresses after that, but none of them looked nice on her customers to be considered as a launch of new trend in the market. She experimented with corsets, denim, flare dresses etc. None of it worked. One of her most loyal customers told her that "you may not be a trend setter, but your dresses are what I wear every day and I love it". Her brand manager also nodded and told Usha that she is best in what she does- Comfort and Elegance are your strengths. Eventually she agreed to it.

She took everyone's feedback and suggestions about each of the dresses diligently. In five years, she launched her own fashion brand and became a renowned fashion designer. Feedback does wonders if one is looking to improve as in the case of Usha.

Regular feedback is a valuable tool for enhancing efficiency in the workplace. Constructive feedback provides individuals and teams with insights into their performance, promotes continuous improvement, and contributes to a positive and productive work environment. When working in a team, provide constructive feedback to team members to help them improve and encourage open communication to address any challenges or concerns.

Here are strategies for incorporating regular feedback to enhance efficiency:

Establish a Feedback Culture: Cultivate a culture where giving and receiving feedback is the norm. Encourage open communication and create an environment where feedback is viewed as a tool for growth rather than criticism.

Frequent Check-Ins: Conduct regular one-on-one or team check-ins to discuss progress, challenges, and goals. These frequent discussions allow for timely feedback and alignment on expectations.

Set Clear Expectations: Clearly define expectations for tasks, projects, and roles. When expectations are well-understood, feedback becomes more specific and actionable.

Feedback Loops: Establish feedback loops within processes or projects. Regularly review and assess progress and provide feedback at key milestones to ensure continuous improvement.

Timely Feedback: Provide feedback promptly after observing performance or completion of a task. Timely feedback allows individuals to make adjustments in real-time, preventing the reinforcement of undesired behaviours.

Balance Positive and Constructive Feedback: Maintain a balance between positive reinforcement and constructive criticism. Recognize achievements and strengths, and provide guidance on areas for improvement.

Use Specific Examples: When giving feedback, use specific examples to illustrate your points. Concrete examples make the feedback more actionable and help individuals understand the context.

Encourage Self-Assessment: Encourage individuals to self-assess their performance. This reflection can lead to more insightful discussions during feedback sessions and fosters a sense of ownership in improvement efforts.

360-Degree Feedback: Implement 360-degree feedback, where individuals receive input from peers, subordinates, and supervisors. This comprehensive approach provides a holistic view of performance.

Goal Alignment: Align feedback with individual and organizational goals. Connect feedback to the broader context of personal and professional development, ensuring that it contributes to overarching objectives.

Encourage Peer Feedback: Foster a culture of peer feedback where team members provide constructive input to one another. Peer perspectives can offer unique insights and contribute to a collaborative work environment.

Use a Growth Mindset: Approach feedback with a growth mindset. Emphasize that feedback is an opportunity for learning and improvement, not a judgment of one's abilities.

Performance Metrics: Establish clear performance metrics and use them as a basis for feedback. Objective metrics provide a measurable foundation for discussions and improvement plans.

Feedback Training: Provide training on giving and receiving feedback effectively. Equip team members with the skills to communicate feedback in a constructive and respectful manner.

Continuous Improvement Plans: Collaboratively develop improvement plans based on feedback. Outline specific actions, milestones, and timelines to address areas for development.

Feedback Surveys: Periodically conduct feedback surveys to gather anonymous input from team members. Surveys can uncover broader trends and provide insights into organizational dynamics.

Acknowledge Efforts: Acknowledge and appreciate individuals' efforts in implementing feedback. Positive reinforcement reinforces the importance of learning and growth.

Regular feedback, when delivered thoughtfully and constructively, contributes to a culture of continuous improvement and efficiency in the workplace. It empowers individuals and teams to excel, adapt, and thrive in dynamic work environments.

TECHNOLOGY

Use Technology Wisely

Nyra works as Master Event Planner. Her work revolves around managing on-going events and planning for upcoming events. Every event is different from the other. One could be Wedding party, the other could be a Book Launch event or a New Year party. The type differs and so does the requirements.

Nyra has been able to fulfil all the deliverable using some of the best planning tools available in the market. One such example is a "To-do" list. She uses it often and never forgets even a minor item.

Utilizing technology effectively is instrumental in enhancing efficiency across various aspects of work and life. Also, stay organized with project management and collaboration tools.

Here are several areas where technology can be applied to increase efficiency:

Project Management Tools: Platforms like Trello, Asana, or Jira help streamline project management by facilitating task organization, collaboration, and tracking progress. These tools enhance communication and coordination within teams.

Communication and Collaboration Platforms: Tools such as Slack, Microsoft Teams, or Zoom enable efficient communication and collaboration, particularly in remote or distributed work environments. They provide instant messaging, video conferencing, file sharing, and project collaboration features.

Cloud Computing: Cloud platforms like AWS, Google Cloud, and Microsoft Azure provide scalable and accessible computing resources. Cloud computing enhances efficiency by enabling remote access to data, applications, and services.

Automation Software: Automation tools, such as Zapier, Microsoft Power Automate, or IFTTT, allow the automation of repetitive tasks across various applications. Automation minimizes manual effort, reduces errors, and increases overall efficiency.

Customer Relationship Management (CRM) Systems: CRM systems like Salesforce or HubSpot help manage customer interactions and streamline sales and marketing processes. They improve efficiency by organizing customer data, automating workflows, and enhancing communication.

Time Tracking and Management Apps: Apps like Toggl, RescueTime, or Clockify help individuals and teams track time spent on tasks. Time management tools contribute to improved productivity by providing insights into time allocation and identifying areas for optimization.

Collaborative Document Editing: Platforms like Google Workspace and Microsoft Office 365 facilitate real-time collaborative editing of documents, spreadsheets, and presentations. This ensures that multiple team members can work on the same document simultaneously.

Task Management Apps: Apps like Todoist, Wunderlist, or Microsoft To Do help organize and prioritize tasks. Task management tools enhance efficiency by providing a structured approach to managing workload and deadlines.

Digital Note-Taking Apps: Apps like Evernote, OneNote, or Notion enable users to take and organize digital notes. These tools enhance efficiency by offering easy access to information, collaboration features, and search capabilities.

E-learning Platforms: Platforms like Coursera, Udemy, or LinkedIn Learning provide opportunities for continuous learning. E-learning enhances efficiency by allowing individuals to acquire new skills at their own pace, often without the need for traditional classroom settings.

Expense Management Software: Tools like Expensify or Concur automate the expense tracking and reimbursement process. Expense management software enhances efficiency by reducing manual data entry and streamlining the approval workflow.

Data Analytics and Business Intelligence Tools: Tools like Tableau, Power BI, or Google Data Studio help analyze and visualize data. Data analytics tools enhance efficiency by providing insights into business performance and supporting data-driven decision-making.

Virtual Assistants and Chatbots: Virtual assistants like Siri, Google Assistant, or chatbots on websites provide quick information and support. They contribute to efficiency by automating routine queries and tasks.

Cybersecurity Solutions: Security tools and solutions, such as antivirus software, firewalls, and VPNs, protect digital assets and sensitive information. Cybersecurity measures enhance efficiency by safeguarding against potential threats and ensuring data integrity.

Mobile Productivity Apps: Productivity apps for mobile devices, such as Microsoft Office apps, Google Drive, or task management apps, allow users to work efficiently on the go.

Integrated Software Suites: Integrated suites like Microsoft 365 or Google Workspace combine multiple productivity tools into a unified platform, promoting seamless collaboration and efficiency.

When strategically implemented, technology can significantly contribute to increased efficiency, streamlined processes, and improved overall productivity in various professional and personal contexts.

WORKSPACE

Optimize Workspace

Ranvijay is a high school student. His study room was a mess. His study table was even more unorganized. Seeing the mess, he use to often lie down on the sofa or couch to study.

Soon he started developing pain on his neck and shoulder due to increased pressure while lying down. He was advised to go for an ergonomic assignment. With the help of the assessment, he realised that using study table and adjusting the chair properly would help him correct his posture and reduce body pain. Understanding that, he cleared the clutter from his table and room. All this helped him to correct his posture, reduce pain and gave him a wonderful atmosphere to study. Thereby increasing his performance at school.

Optimizing your workspace is crucial for achieving efficiency and maintaining a productive and organized environment. Ensure a comfortable and organized workspace to minimize distractions. Consider the ergonomics of your workspace for improved physical comfort.

Here are practical tips to help you optimize your workspace:

Declutter and Organize: Start by decluttering your workspace. Remove unnecessary items and organize your desk, drawers, and storage spaces. A clean and organized environment promotes focus and reduces distractions.

Prioritize Essentials: Identify and prioritize essential items on your desk. Keep only the tools and materials you use regularly within arm's reach. Store less frequently used items in designated areas.

Ergonomic Setup: Arrange your desk and chair to create an ergonomic workspace. Ensure that your computer screen is at eye level, your chair provides proper support, and your keyboard and mouse are easily accessible.

Proper Lighting: Ensure adequate lighting in your workspace. Natural light is ideal, but if that's not possible, use well-positioned artificial lighting to reduce eye strain and create a comfortable working environment.

Use Cable Management: Keep cables organized and out of sight. Use cable organizers, clips, or cable sleeves to prevent tangled cords. This not only improves the aesthetics but also makes it easier to clean and maintain the workspace.

Personalize Thoughtfully: Add personal touches to your workspace, but do so thoughtfully. Consider incorporating plants, artwork, or motivational quotes to create a positive and inspiring atmosphere without overwhelming the space.

Effective Storage Solutions: Invest in efficient storage solutions such as shelves, cabinets, or drawer organizers. Group similar items together and label storage containers for easy access and retrieval.

Digital Organization: Organize your digital files on your computer. Use folders and a consistent naming convention to keep files easily accessible. Regularly clean up and archive files you no longer need.

Task-specific Zones: Create dedicated zones for specific tasks. For example, have a zone for focused work, a separate area for meetings or calls, and a designated spot for breaks. This helps in mentally switching between different work modes.

Dual Monitors: If possible, use dual monitors to increase your screen real estate. This can enhance multitasking and productivity by allowing you to view multiple applications simultaneously.

Minimize Distractions: Identify and minimize potential distractions in your workspace. Position your desk away from high-traffic areas, use noise-cancelling headphones, or establish boundaries with colleagues during focused work periods.

Inbox Management: Keep your physical and digital inboxes organized. Process emails and physical mail regularly, categorize them, and prioritize tasks associated with them.

Comfortable Seating: Invest in a comfortable and supportive chair. Your seating should promote good posture and prevent discomfort during long periods of work.

Regular Maintenance: Schedule regular maintenance sessions to keep your workspace organized. Take a few minutes each day to tidy up and address any clutter that may accumulate.

Mobile Organization: If you work with mobile devices, keep them organized too. Use folders and apps to group similar tasks or tools, and regularly clean up unnecessary apps or files.

Time Management Tools: Utilize tools like calendars, planners, or task management apps to organize and schedule your daily activities. Set reminders for important deadlines and prioritize tasks accordingly.

Reflect and Adjust: Periodically assess the effectiveness of your workspace organization. Consider what is working well and what could be improved. Make adjustments based on changes in your workflow or job requirements.

By optimizing your workspace, you create a conducive environment for productivity and efficiency. Tailor these tips to suit your preferences and work style, and regularly reassess and make adjustments as needed.

Culture

Encourage a Positive Culture

Uttam is a Manager with an Insurance Advisory Firm. He has been awarded "Best Manager of the Year" and his team is considered the best to work for. For three consecutive years, his team has published wonderful ideas, written numerous blogs and created many training materials. All this has been done apart from the wonderful Project work each of them works on.

Uttam often conducts outings and tries newer ways to connect with his team. He keeps the communication channel open. Takes timely feedback from his team and encourages them to help each other. He takes their suggestions positively and asks them to be hands-on. All this helps to build an amazing culture within the team. This helps with enhancing their overall productivity.

Fostering a positive culture in the workplace is a key factor in increasing efficiency. When employees feel valued, motivated, and engaged, they are more likely to contribute their best efforts and work collaboratively. To boost morale, recognize and reward achievements.

Here are strategies to encourage a positive culture for enhanced efficiency:

Open Communication: Cultivate a culture of open and transparent communication. Encourage employees to share their thoughts, ideas, and concerns without fear of reprisal. Actively listen to feedback and address issues promptly.

Recognition and Appreciation: Acknowledge and appreciate employees for their contributions. Regularly recognize individual and team achievements to reinforce a positive and supportive work environment.

Employee Empowerment: Empower employees by providing them with autonomy and decision-making opportunities within their roles. This fosters a sense of ownership and responsibility, leading to increased efficiency.

Clear Expectations: Clearly communicate expectations regarding roles, responsibilities, and performance standards. When employees understand what is expected of them, they can work more efficiently towards meeting those expectations.

Collaborative Environment: Foster a collaborative and team-oriented environment. Encourage teamwork, cross-functional collaboration, and the sharing of knowledge and resources. A collaborative culture promotes efficiency by leveraging collective strengths.

Flexibility and Work-Life Balance: Support flexibility in work arrangements and prioritize work-life balance. Recognize that employees have personal lives and commitments, and offer flexibility when possible. A healthy work-life balance contributes to employee well-being and productivity.

Professional Development Opportunities: Provide opportunities for professional growth and development. This can include training programs, workshops, and mentorship opportunities. Investing in employees' development enhances job satisfaction and efficiency.

Promote Well-being: Prioritize employee well-being by promoting a healthy workplace. Encourage breaks, physical activity, and wellness initiatives. A physically and mentally healthy workforce is more likely to be efficient and engaged.

Inclusive Practices: Embrace diversity and inclusion. Ensure that all employees feel valued and included in the workplace. A diverse and inclusive culture fosters creativity, innovation, and improved problem-solving, contributing to efficiency.

Regular Team Building Activities: Organize regular team-building activities to strengthen relationships among team members. Team building fosters a positive and collaborative atmosphere, leading to increased efficiency in group projects.

Trust and Empathy: Build a culture of trust and empathy. Trust enables smoother collaboration, while empathy fosters understanding and support among colleagues. A trusting and empathetic environment promotes efficient teamwork.

Leadership by Example: Leaders play a crucial role in shaping organizational culture. Lead by example, demonstrating positive behaviours, a strong work ethic, and a commitment to the well-being of your team.

Celebrate Milestones: Celebrate both personal and professional milestones, whether they're work anniversaries, project completions, or personal achievements. Recognition of milestones contributes to a positive and motivating atmosphere.

Continuous Improvement Mindset: Encourage a mindset of continuous improvement. Foster a culture where employees feel empowered to suggest and implement process improvements. This cultivates an environment of innovation and efficiency.

Feedback and Improvement: Establish a feedback loop for continuous improvement. Regularly seek input from employees on how processes and workflows can be enhanced. Act on feedback to demonstrate a commitment to improvement.

Fun and Enjoyable Environment: Create a work environment that is enjoyable and fun. Inject humor, organize team-building games, or set up recreational spaces. A positive and enjoyable workplace enhances morale and efficiency.

By promoting a positive culture that values communication, collaboration, well-being, and continuous improvement, you can create a work environment where employees are motivated to work efficiently and contribute to the success of the organization.

Say 'NO'

Learn to Say "No"

Neha works as an Accountant in a Banking firm. She is considered hardworking, humble, and approachable. She is liked by all her colleagues.

One day, a colleague of hers falls sick. Neha's manager approached her to fill in for Roma, who was sick. Neha had a lot of work of her own, but she could not deny. She felt tired at the end of the day. Soon, the manager started asking Neha to fill in for anyone who had trouble or take up voluntary activities. This affected her mentally and physically. Her own performance started to drop as she no longer liked to work there. However, she was not able to convey the problem to her manager.

Learning to say "no" is a crucial skill for increasing efficiency, maintaining focus, and avoiding burnout. Understand your limits and be willing to say no to tasks that don't align with priorities. Focus on tasks that contribute directly to your goals.

Here are tips on how to effectively say "no" in both personal and professional contexts:

Prioritize Your Goals: Clearly define your goals and priorities. Knowing what is most important to you will help you make informed decisions about where to direct your time and energy.

Understand Your Limits: Be aware of your capacity and limitations. Understanding how much you can realistically take on will prevent you from overcommitting and ensure that you can deliver quality work.

Evaluate Requests: Assess each request or opportunity before agreeing to it. Consider how it aligns with your goals, whether you have the time and resources to fulfill it, and the potential impact on your current commitments.

Be Honest and Direct: When declining a request, be honest and direct. Clearly communicate your reasons for saying "no" without over-explaining or providing excessive details.

Use a Polite Tone: Maintain a polite and respectful tone when saying "no." Express gratitude for the opportunity or request and make it clear that your decision is based on your current priorities and workload.

Offer Alternatives: If possible, suggest alternatives or compromises. This shows your willingness to help in a different capacity or at a later time, demonstrating a positive and collaborative attitude.

Practice Assertiveness: Practice assertiveness in your communication. It's okay to set boundaries and protect your time. Remember that saying "no" is not a negative action but a strategic decision to manage your commitments effectively.

Use Time Management Techniques: Implement time management techniques, such as setting realistic deadlines, prioritizing tasks, and blocking focused work periods. This helps you manage your time more effectively and reduces the need to decline requests.

Learn to Delegate: Delegate tasks when possible. If someone else is better suited to handle a particular task or project, consider passing it on to them. Delegating effectively can help lighten your workload.

Create a Schedule: Establish a schedule that includes dedicated time for important tasks and activities. Having a structured schedule makes it easier to assess your availability and make informed decisions about additional commitments.

Stay Firm but Polite: Be firm in your decision to say "no," but maintain a polite and respectful demeanour. It's important to stand by your boundaries without causing unnecessary conflict.

Focus on Quality, Not Quantity: Emphasize the quality of your work over the quantity of tasks you take on. Prioritize projects that align with your expertise and contribute significantly to your goals.

Learn to Say "No" to Yourself: Recognize the importance of saying "no" to your own impulses and distractions. Be disciplined in adhering to your priorities and avoiding activities that deviate from your goals.

Set Clear Expectations: Clearly communicate your availability and set realistic expectations with colleagues, friends, or family. Setting clear boundaries helps others understand your capacity.

Reflect on Past Commitments: Reflect on past commitments and assess the impact of overcommitting on your well-being and performance. Use these reflections to inform future decisions.

Remember that saying "no" is not a rejection of others but a strategic decision to protect your time and energy. It's an essential skill for maintaining balance, achieving your goals, and ensuring that your contributions are meaningful and effective.

EVALUATE AND

ADJUST

Regularly Evaluate and Adjust

Gaurav owns a Gaming company. His games are well known for visuals, processing speed and innovation. He wants his firm to be the "Best Gaming Company" with games for all ages. He wishes to cater to all ages of gamers.

After few years, he thought of venturing into e-commerce sector which was booming at that time. He had thought both games and e-commerce business is manageable. However, he was utterly wrong. E-commerce is all about right product, available at the right time to the customer. Customer is the king and centric to all the future demands and Customer Service needs to be best. He started incurring losses and reassessed his companies long term goals. He realised that he had deviated from his goal. He corrected his actions and sold the E-commerce division. He started focusing on 2D, 3D and AI based games. Thereby once again known to be the Best Games company in the market.

Regularly evaluating and adjusting your approach, strategies, and priorities is essential for increasing efficiency. Continuous improvement requires a willingness to reflect on your methods, identify areas for enhancement, and adapt to changing circumstances. Be open to feedback and continuous improvement.

Here's a guide on how to regularly evaluate and adjust to optimize efficiency:

Set Clear Goals: Begin with clear and specific goals. Regularly assess whether your current goals align with your overall objectives. Adjust them if necessary to stay focused on what truly matters.

Establish Key Performance Indicators (KPIs): Define measurable KPIs that align with your goals. Regularly evaluate your performance against these indicators to gauge your progress and identify areas that need improvement.

Frequent Self-Reflection: Take time for regular self-reflection. Assess your strengths, weaknesses, and areas for improvement. Identify habits or practices that contribute to efficiency as well as those that hinder it.

Feedback from Others: Seek feedback from colleagues, supervisors, or team members. External perspectives can provide valuable insights into your work and help identify blind spots. Use constructive feedback as a basis for adjustments.

Performance Metrics: Establish performance metrics for your tasks and projects. Regularly review these metrics to identify trends, patterns, and opportunities for optimization. Adjust your approach based on the insights gained.

Time Tracking: Use time-tracking tools to monitor how you allocate your time. Analyze the data to identify time-consuming activities or inefficiencies. Adjust your schedule to prioritize high-impact tasks.

Evaluate Work Processes: Regularly assess your work processes. Identify bottlenecks, redundancies, or steps that can be streamlined. Implement changes to enhance the efficiency of your workflows.

Stay Informed About Industry Trends: Stay updated on industry trends, best practices, and new technologies. Regularly evaluate whether your current methods are aligned with the latest advancements. Embrace innovations that can improve efficiency.

Flexibility and Adaptability: Cultivate a mindset of flexibility and adaptability. Be open to adjusting your plans when unexpected challenges arise. The ability to pivot in response to changing circumstances is key to maintaining efficiency.

Regularly Review Priorities: Prioritize tasks based on their impact and urgency. Regularly review and adjust your priorities to align with changing goals, deadlines, or project requirements.

Evaluate Collaborative Efforts: If you work in a team, regularly evaluate the effectiveness of collaborative efforts. Assess communication, coordination, and the overall team dynamic. Adjust collaboration strategies as needed.

Audit and Clean Up: Conduct regular audits of your digital and physical workspaces. Remove unnecessary files, declutter your environment, and organize materials. A clean and organized space contributes to improved efficiency.

Embrace Continuous Learning: Stay committed to continuous learning. Regularly seek new knowledge and skills relevant to your field. Apply what you learn to optimize your work processes and stay ahead of industry developments.

Assess Work-Life Balance: Evaluate your work-life balance regularly. Ensure that you are maintaining a healthy equilibrium between work and personal life. Adjust your schedule or priorities if needed to prevent burnout.

Celebrate Successes and Learn from Failures: Celebrate your successes and achievements. Likewise, learn from failures and setbacks. Regularly assess what worked well and what didn't, and use these insights to refine your approach.

Adjust Based on Feedback: Act on feedback received from colleagues, clients, or customers. Adjust your strategies and behaviours based on constructive input to enhance your overall efficiency.

Regularly Update Professional Development Plans: Review and update your professional development plans regularly. Identify new skills or knowledge areas that can contribute to your efficiency. Adjust your learning goals accordingly.

Evaluate Tools and Technologies: Assess the effectiveness of the tools and technologies you use. Regularly review whether they still meet your needs or if there are more efficient alternatives available. Embrace new tools that can enhance your workflows.

Regular evaluation and adjustment are fundamental to continuous improvement and increased efficiency. By staying vigilant, proactive, and open to change, you can adapt to evolving circumstances and optimize your performance over time.

Summary

Increasing efficiency at work involves adopting strategies and practices that help you and your team accomplish more in less time. Here are some tips to enhance efficiency in the workplace:

1. **Set Clear Goals and Prioritize Tasks:**

- Clearly define your goals and objectives.

- Prioritize tasks based on urgency and importance.

2. **Time Management:**

- Use tools like calendars, planners, or productivity apps to schedule and track your time.

- Break down larger tasks into smaller, more manageable chunks.

3. **Eliminate Distractions:**

- Identify and minimize distractions such as unnecessary meetings, notifications, or social media.

- Consider implementing focused work periods without interruptions.

4. **Delegate Responsibility:**

- Delegate tasks to team members based on their strengths and expertise.

- Trust your team and empower them to take ownership of their responsibilities.

5.   Improve Communication:

- Use clear and concise communication methods.

- Utilize project management tools and collaboration platforms to streamline communication.

6.   Automate Repetitive Tasks:

- Identify repetitive and time-consuming tasks that can be automated.

- Explore tools and software that can help automate routine processes.

7.   Continuous Learning:

- Stay updated on the latest tools and techniques in your field.

- Encourage a culture of continuous learning within your team.

8.   Streamline Meetings:

- Keep meetings focused and have a clear agenda.

- Only invite necessary participants to avoid wasting time.

9.   Encourage Breaks and Rest:

- Short breaks can help refresh the mind and increase overall productivity.

- Encourage a healthy work-life balance to prevent burnout.

10.   Regular Feedback:

- Provide constructive feedback to team members to help them improve.

- Encourage open communication to address any challenges or concerns.

11.   Use Technology Wisely:

•   Leverage technology tools that enhance productivity and communication.

•   Stay organized with project management and collaboration tools.

12.   Optimize Workspace:

•   Ensure a comfortable and organized workspace to minimize distractions.

•   Consider the ergonomics of your workspace for improved physical comfort.

13.   Encourage a Positive Culture:

•   Foster a positive and collaborative work environment.

•   Recognize and reward achievements to boost morale.

14.   Learn to Say No:

•   Understand your limits and be willing to say no to tasks that don't align with priorities.

•   Focus on tasks that contribute directly to your goals.

15.   Regularly Evaluate and Adjust:

•   Assess your workflow periodically and make adjustments as needed.

•   Be open to feedback and continuous improvement.

By implementing these strategies, you can create a more efficient work environment and increase productivity for yourself and your team.

About the Author

Ram Asare Shukla

Ram Asare Shukla is retired from Indian Air Force. He likes to read in his leisure time. Learning, Teaching, and imparting knowledge has been the essence of his life. He is passionate about education. He believes the world can be better place if everyone is educated and do their work dedicatedly. He is punctual and likes to be the best at whatever work he does. He has taken multiple leadership roles during his service years.

In his course of service and even post retirement Ram always felt that each task that is either at workplace or at home can be completed faster over time. He likes to explore newer ways to do the same repetitive tasks. He likes to help others with achieving more in lesser time.

9 798889 065354